TRACK
CHRISTIAN
LIFE

EDWARD T. WELCH

A STUDENT'S GUIDE TO

ANXIETY

D1634953

CHRISTIAN
FOCUS

rȝm

Scripture quotations are from *The Holy Bible, English Standard Version*, copyright © 2001 by Crossway Bibles, a publishing ministry of Good News Publishers. Used by permission. All rights reserved. ESV Text Edition: 2011.

Scripture quotations taken from the *Holy Bible, New International Version*®, NIV® Copyright © 1973, 1978, 1984, 2011 by Biblica, Inc.™ Used by permission. All rights reserved worldwide.

Copyright © Edward T. Welch 2020

paperback ISBN 978-1-5271-0450-1
epub ISBN 978-1-5271-0547-8
mobi ISBN 978-1-5271-0548-5

10 9 8 7 6 5 4 3 2 1

First published in 2020
by
Christian Focus Publications Ltd,
Geanies House, Fearn, Ross-shire,
IV20 1TW, Great Britain

www.christianfocus.com

with

Reformed Youth Ministries,
1445 Rio Road East
Suite 201D
Charlottesville,
Virginia, 22911

Cover by MOOSE77

Printed by Gutenberg, Malta

One of my favorite classes in seminary was my Biblical counseling class. After hearing my professor open both the Scriptures and the human heart and apply the former to the latter, I determined that if I could preach like anyone I wanted it be a Biblical counselor. Ed Welch is one of the church's foremost counselors, and this book will help you not only understand your own heart, but the hearts of those you love. Dr. Welch's books have been immensely helpful to me, and this book is no exception.

J.D. Greear
Pastor, The Summit Church, Raleigh-Durham, North Carolina
62nd President, The Southern Baptist Convention
Author of several books

This is a book about you, about something you face every day. Ed Welch gets that every single one of us struggles with anxiety and this book is incredibly accessible. Reading this will help you identify and deal with the core of your anxieties, and it gives answers that are not bandaids or simplistic. This book is perfect for teens trying to understand where their anxiety comes from, but be careful parents, it might have more to say to you than you expect!

Alasdair Groves
Executive Director of CCEF

Our risk-averse society with its prophecies of doom is a breeding-ground for anxiety, not least among children and teens. Ed Welch here offers young people a means to understand the roots of their own fears and discover how to live every day with genuine hope.

Ann Benton
Author and family conference speaker

I've read many books and articles that analyze the causes of the current epidemic of anxiety among teenagers, but few of them get beyond superficial and temporary cures. In this little book, Ed Welch provides big biblical solutions that get to the heart of the matter and that last. It rejoices my heart to think of all the students that will have their lives transformed by the truths in these pages.

David Murray
Professor of Old Testament and Practical Theology,
Puritan Reformed Seminary, Grand Rapids, Michigan
Author of *Christians Get Depressed Too* and
Reset: Living a Grace-Paced Life in a Burnout Culture

CONTENTS

Series Introduction

Christianity is a religion of words, because our God is a God of words. He created through words, calls Himself the Living Word, and wrote a book (filled with words) to communicate to His children. In light of this, pastors and parents should take great efforts to train the next generation to be readers; *Track* is a series designed to do exactly that.

Written for students, the *Track* series addresses a host of topics in three primary areas: Doctrine, Culture, & the Christian Life. *Track's* booklets are theologically rich, yet accessible. They seek to engage and challenge the student without dumbing things down.

One definition of a track reads, *a way that has been formed by someone else's footsteps.* The goal of the *Track* series is to point us to that 'someone else' – Jesus Christ. The One who forged a track to guide His followers. While we cannot follow this track perfectly, by His grace and Spirit He calls us to strive to stay on the path. It is our prayer that this series of booklets would help guide Christ's Church until He returns.

In His Service,

John Perritt
RYM's Director of Resources
Series Editor

1. This is Really Important

Everyone has fears and anxieties. You might have a moment when all seems well. Life is good. You can manage. But those moments don't last long before reality creeps in. Homework needs to be done, you got embarrassed in Algebra class, your ex started dating your friend, and your future has no guarantees. While you are at it, you might go big and fret about your future—which college to attend, who you're going to marry. Or, even bigger thoughts that have a broader impact—global warming or terrorism. All of a sudden, your life seems to be unraveling. Life becomes chaos.

Anxiety is no longer just a problem for older people with their kids, car payments, and a long list of responsibilities. It is true that adults have plenty of anxieties—opportunities for anxieties *will* grow as you get older, of that you can be sure—but now they have settled into your school and friend group. So now is a good time to take a look.

You have good reasons for a careful look. Though a visit to your anxieties would seem to run the risk of making you more anxious, you are doing this for at least two reasons:

1. Anxiety and fear are big problems. They wrap around most everything you do. You have to do *something* with them.
2. God singles out anxious and fearful people for His most encouraging and beautiful words. It would be sad if you missed them.

The first step is to find your fears and anxieties and put them into words. Maybe a conversation with a friend would help. Since everyone struggles with these things, your friends should be willing to listen.

There are lots of words for worries and anxieties. All of them say the same thing— you think bad things are going to happen to something important to you. Here are some of those words.

Anxiety can be like background noise that follows you through the day. The bad thing might not be happening yet, but you believe it will. You can feel it coming.

Worry is anxiety that is not freaking out *yet*.

Fear is when a bad thing is especially close.

Stress or **pressure** means that daily life is too much for you. Too many tests, quizzes, practices, and relationships. There are too many places where you could fail. Bad things are up ahead.

Nervous, jittery, tense, a racing mind, on edge, panicky, freaking out, dread—these are a few other words. You get the idea.

Now go a little further.

Have you seen any horror movies? It seems strange that they are so popular. Why add to your fear and anxiety? Perhaps they serve a different purpose. They put words and images on what we already feel. We *feel* vulnerable and unsafe, and horror movies assure us that we are, indeed, unsafe, while watching them in the comfort of our own living room or crowded theater.

You make decisions every day, and they affect your future. If you say 'yes' to one thing, you have just said 'no' to many others. FOMO. You have just re-directed the course of your life. Who knows what you might miss out on?

Someone you know has had panic attacks. *Many* people you know have had panic attacks. These feel as if all your anxieties were dumped on you, all at once, without any warning, and your body can't take it.

Everybody has specific fears: public speaking, snakes, bugs, germs, tests, planes and other places that you can't easily escape.

Depression, even suicide, usually contains anxieties about the future. You feel trapped in pain, and you predict that it will never get better.

Social media guarantees anxiety. You compare yourself to others, and you are putting yourself out in public. Who knows what other people might say about you?

The fear of failure. Not measuring up to those around you. Not being really good at something. You don't have to look far for this one.

Every relationship comes packaged with the fear of rejection. You can't escape this one.

Drugs and alcohol are all around. For many people, they are ways to relieve the pressures and worries of life.

Is there anything in your life that you want to hide? A life that hides or lies will be an anxious life.

Now add worries about family members, what kind of job you want, shootings and most world news.

And this is only a warm up.

Anxiety is a prediction: something important to you—a relationship, your parent's marriage, your reputation, your being included, your life, your family, your vocational track—is in trouble. It is a prediction that something will end badly.

'*Will* I get a good grade?' Your prediction: 'Absolutely not.'

'*Will* that person like me?' No.

'*Will* anyone talk to me?' Never.

'*Will* I be invited?' Nobody likes me.

You feel your worries and anxieties *now*, but they are telling stories about your future. **The trick is to focus on today more than tomorrow**. More on that later. For now, you have enough to do: just find them. Put words on your fears, anxieties, stresses and worries. You can't do much with them unless you find them and give them a name. Chances are, once you identify one, you will see dozens. Human beings are small. We have less power than we think. The world is dangerous. *Everyone* has fears and anxieties.

Everyone.

We will start by looking at things that are hard, which might be a little uncomfortable, but I hope you will like the journey. Let's get started.

Main Point

We all need to decide how to deal with our anxieties.

Questions for Reflection

- Where do you see anxiety, fear or worry in your life? Where do you find it at home? School? Church?
- Try to listen to these anxieties. What are they saying?
- Human beings are not intended to be islands. Tell someone else that you are thinking about worries and anxiety. Start with your parents, mentors, youth workers, or pastor. You'll probably discover they all struggled—or are still struggling with these today.
- Take comfort that you're not alone.

2. The Lord is Near You

When the right person is with you, you have more courage. Imagine a movie scene in which all hope seems lost and the hero is fighting with his last ounce of strength. The enemy is too strong. You can see the anxiety on his face. It is just a matter of time before all is lost.

Then he feels something. The ground beneath him comes alive. He hears rumbling. Hoofbeats. The neighboring kings have banded together and are coming to the rescue with a vast army. Anxiety vanishes. Courage takes its place. The army is not there yet, but they will be soon, and the hero will be delivered. His strength returns. The enemy flees.

Great stories. Too bad that most of them are fantasies. But there is one story …

GOD IS WITH YOU

These images can actually be found in the book of Revelation. They were borrowed by *The Lord of the Rings* and many other movies. But the original story is true. They are about you and the God who is very near you, who hears, and who acts.

God is with you, and He usually brings an army of angels with Him.

Since His presence is hard to see, God promises you that He is near. And He makes that promise to you again and again because you probably won't believe Him the first ten times. This is what He says:

Do not be afraid, for I am with you. (Gen. 26:24, NIV)

Do not be afraid or terrified because of them, for the LORD your God goes with you wherever you go; he will never leave you or forsake you. (Deut. 31:6, NIV)

I will not forget you! See, I have engraved you on the palms of my hands. (Isa. 49:15-16)

I will never leave you nor forsake you. (Heb. 13:5)

And on and on. Think about people who love each other. They are always saying, 'I love you.' They can't help themselves. They want to say it. They like to say it.

God *likes* to tell you that He is close. He *wants* to be close to you. He made you to be close to Him. This is how He expresses His love, and this just happens to be the most important way He speaks to you about your worries.

Yes, this can be *really* hard to believe, so be careful to listen.

Listening to God is not always easy. Instead of speaking to you with a voice you can hear, He speaks to you in writing, as in a personal letter or a long text message. But that is not the hard part.

Here is the problem. When life is okay and you feel like things are under control, you don't need Him. When you don't need Him, you don't bother reading the Bible or listening to Him. Then, when life gets crazy, you think He is far away because you haven't learned how to listen to Him. You forget about His texts. You think they have no answers. So you try to control your own life. You get frantic. You feel out of control. You fall apart. Does this describe you? Either way, when things are good or bad, listening is not easy.

Anxiety and worry are a reminder to listen. That's your mission.

Your anxiety reminds you that you need Him, so anxiety is not as bad as you think. When you read the New Testament, Jesus always had time for those who knew they needed Him. Both Jesus and His Father are glad to be needed. (Most parents are glad to be needed too.)

FAITH AND ANXIETY

Eyes that see, ears that hear. So it is time to hear more and see more. The Bible calls this faith. It is a gift that God gives to those who ask. What is faith? Faith is like glasses that God gives to help you see more clearly. Faith is earbuds that help you hear more than you can with your ordinary ears. God speaks to you in the Bible and His words open your eyes to see and your ears to hear.

Here is how faith works.

Look around you. You see life and light everywhere.

Listen more carefully. God has told you that He created all things.

Look around again—by faith—and you will see the artist behind it all. Life is everywhere because God is the Life. Light is essential for life and peace. It comes because God Himself is the Light.

Now look at Jesus. You see a historical figure who changed history in three short years.

Look and listen more carefully, and see Him by faith. No one else has ever calmed a storm with a word or touched the eyes of the blind and they could see. Jesus is God Himself. Listen to the New Testament letters and there is more. He was the lamb who, from the beginning of time, planned to come to rescue you and bring you to Himself. Your sins and lack of interest in him separated you from Him. His death took the penalty for your sin so that nothing could ever separate you from Him again. His death for sin is the reason why He can be near you. His resurrection is why the stories from the Bible are about the *living* God, not just a historical person.

Now try one more. When you look around, you can see all kinds of dangers, and most of them are very real. Sickness, tragedy, divorce, and death. But when you look and listen by faith, you can see more. You can see that God is near.

CAN YOU SEE GOD?

There was a time when there was a king of Israel, Elisha was a prophet, and Syria was an enemy. God aided Israel by revealing to Elisha all the plans of the king of Syria. Whatever the king said in secret, Elisha told the Israelite army, so Israel was always one step ahead of its Syrian enemy. When the king of Syria learned that Elisha was the culprit, he sent out his army to capture him.

Elisha's servant was up early and saw that they were surrounded.

When the servant of the man of God rose early in the morning and went out, behold, an army with horses and chariots was all around the city. And the servant said, 'Alas, my master! What shall we do?' He said, 'Do not be afraid, for those who are with us are more than those who are with them.' Then Elisha prayed and said, 'O LORD, please open his eyes that he may see.' So the LORD opened the eyes of the young man, and he saw, and behold, the mountain was full of horses and chariots of fire all around Elisha. (2 Kings 6:15-17)

Elisha could already see by faith. His servant needed help. Elisha told his servant that the army of the Lord was near, and it was much greater than Syria. Then God gave His servant the gift of faith and he could see more.

That would be nice, wouldn't it? If you could just have your eyes opened for a minute and see everything. But the truth is this: it wouldn't help. If you can't see that army by faith right now, you wouldn't see it if God repeated the story right in front of you. Instead, you would immediately forget. Then you would ask Him for *another* sign, and another, and another, and then walk away, blind to the deeper story.

It is hard to see by faith. So ask Jesus to help you see. Ask Him to help you believe. A wise person once said, 'I believe, help my unbelief' (Mark 9:24), and Jesus helped.

Now, it is time to listen for the hoofbeats and see the heavenly armies.

Jesus, help me to believe so that I can see.

Main Point

Anxiety is a reminder to look to Jesus.

Questions for Reflection

- How is your spiritual eyesight?
- What helps you really see? What helps other people you know?
- What reason might you doubt that God is near?

3. Speak to the Lord

In every relationship, you talk. Even text messaging is a form of talking. Less effective at times, but it's communication nonetheless. Total silence is *not* what you do with people you love.

Even infants talk, in their own way. You babbled, cooed and cried. A little later you cried out to a parent when you imagined what could be lurking in the darkness. When you were hurt, you cried out for help. That's just what we do when we feel desperate and someone we love is close by.

Since talking and crying out are so natural, you would think that anxieties and fear would get you talking to the Lord. After all, you feel desperate. You feel as if you can't take it one more second. But you are not as good at crying for help as you once were. It is no longer natural to you. You are older, more independent. You're growing up in a culture that celebrates independence.

Or maybe you feel like an orphan without God as your Father. In orphanages, children no longer cry out when they need something. They have learned that no one will listen to them or pick them up. No one is with them.

But you are not an orphan, and you, like everyone else, are weak, needy and dependent. You cannot protect yourself from the troubles of life. A superpower or two would be nice. But you don't have such things. Instead, you were made to be dependent on other people and dependent on God.

TALKING TO GOD

The most important thing you can do in your life is to say to Jesus, 'Help.' That is faith. Faith means that you need God to rescue, forgive, and bring you to Himself. You need Him to be close.

Did you know that you might be asking for help without even knowing it? Sometimes you're asking for help when you binge-watch videos. You may be asking for help when you scroll endlessly through social media. You see, our anxieties move us to escape this world and we'll often try to fix them through online distractions.

It's not wrong to watch videos online or get on social media, but start to observe your habits and see if this might be the case. Instead of running to these distractions for help, start turning to God.

Worries, stresses and anxieties are the perfect opportunity to learn how to ask for help.

Trust in him at all times, O people; pour out your heart before him. (Ps. 62:8)

'Pour out your heart before him.' This is how life works in God's house. He speaks to you and you speak to Him. You don't keep your worries and anxieties to yourself, no matter how unimportant they might seem. You speak them to someone who cares about you, and God cares about you.

You have probably read or even memorized parts of the psalms. You are familiar with 'The LORD is my shepherd' (Ps. 23:1), even if you never read it. All these psalms are from people who have poured out their heart to the Lord. They speak to Him about their hopes and dreams, they speak about how great the

Lord is, and they speak about everything in life that is hard. They speak about their fears and worries. They speak about what is most important to them.

It *sounds* easy to do. Just start talking.

It is *not* easy to do. We know how to do it but we rarely do. Any ideas why?

- You would have trouble speaking about your worries to **any** adult.
- You don't believe that God wants to speak with you.
- You think that it doesn't matter whether you speak to Him or not.
- You just don't **feel** like it because it seems like it takes too much work.
- Your faith is so tiny you don't hear God's actual voice, you don't see Him, and you can't touch Him. So why bother?

GOD IS SPEAKING AND LISTENING

Throughout your life you will have troubles, some that are more severe than others. When those troubles are overwhelming, and you cry out to the Lord for help, and you think He is silent, you are going to cry out less and less. At some point you might say that you still believe God exists, but you might know people who exist on the other side of the world, and you don't talk to them either.

Here is the truth.

- God is the creator who made tongues and ears because He is the one who speaks and hears. 'While they are yet speaking I will hear' (Isa. 65:24).
- God came to earth in Jesus Christ. The Bible is written by those who saw Him. 'That which was from the beginning [Jesus], which we have heard, which we have seen with our eyes, which we looked upon and have touched with our hands … we proclaim also to you ' (1 John 1:1-3).
- Jesus said something peculiar to Thomas, who wouldn't believe that Jesus rose from the dead unless he could see and touch Him. Jesus said to him, 'Have you believed because you have seen me? Blessed are those who have not seen and yet have believed' (John 20:29). Somehow, your present relationship with Jesus can be better than what Thomas had.
- Jesus is alive today. The one you read about—that same Jesus who promised to hear you—still hears. He is now in heaven in His physical body. A physical body

cannot be everywhere at the same time. So when He ascended to heaven, He sent His Spirit. 'God's love has been poured into our hearts through the Holy Spirit who has been given to us' (Rom. 5:5). The Spirit is Jesus-with-us.

- The Spirit is so uniquely joined with Jesus that He is called the Spirit of Christ (Rom 8:9). If you trust in Jesus for true life rather than yourself, you have the Spirit, which means that you have Jesus.

- The Spirit was the one who linked Jesus with His Father when Jesus was on earth, so He is no second-rate connection. Jesus knew His Father's presence through the Spirit.

This is a lot. By faith you see that Jesus is alive and is with you by the Holy Spirit.

Since He is so close, speak to Him. Simply say, 'Jesus, I need help.'

If you want to say more, you can borrow the words of other men and women of faith. God is pleased when you borrow them.

My heart is in anguish within me; the terrors of death have fallen upon me. Fear and trembling come upon me, and horror overwhelms me. And I say, 'Oh, that I had wings like a dove! I would fly away and be at rest.' (Ps. 55:4-6)

The psalmist wanted to escape what he feared. That should sound familiar. Go ahead and make the psalmist's words your own. Why not pray to God right now? Don't think that you have to say the perfect words. God already knows your heart. So, just go ahead and say something to Him.

Main Point

Anxiety is a reminder to talk to Jesus.

Questions for Reflection

- What helps you see that Jesus is present with you?
- Why is it hard for you to talk to God?
- Did you know that you can say to Him, 'If I could I would fly away'? What other words are you saying to Him?
- Have you asked God to help you talk to Him?

4. God is Loving, God is Strong

'It will be alright.'

Dad was trying to assure his daughter. The presentation she had to give to her class would go just fine.

'You always get nervous before you have to do something like this, and you always do great.'

He was trying to help. He loved his daughter and had confidence in her abilities. But his words didn't make any difference. How did he know she would be alright? He loved her, but he couldn't make her short speech a success. And maybe she did get nervous before public speaking, and things had always gone better than she expected, but that didn't mean that she would do well this time.

Sometimes, assuring words, even from those who love you, can make you feel even more alone. You are glad they love you, but they are just as powerless as you. They can't change your future. This is why God says that He loves you, *and* He says that He is powerful.

I heard this: that power belongs to God, and that to you, O Lord, belongs steadfast love. (Ps. 62:11-12)

This is the right combination for anxious people.

So consider these two questions. Do you believe that He loves you? Do you believe that He is powerful?

A quick 'yes' is not enough. Does He *really* love you? Why would He? And, yes, He is powerful—He created everything—but didn't Jesus usually choose not to use His power? These questions are reasons to go slowly.

DOES HE LOVE YOU?

In school you read to learn information. Or, you just read to get a grade for the class. If you already know the information, you skip over it until you find something new. With the truth about God, you have to read differently. In the Bible, God speaks to you, and you do something with what He says. When you read about World War I, you don't have to do anything. You just get the information and pass the test. When you believe in Jesus you do something.

So slow down. Jesus asks you to listen and see by faith, and then respond.

He says this: Jesus loves you because that is what He does. He is love. He loves you first, before you did or said anything. When you are being selfish, He loves you (2 Tim. 2:13). If He died for you when you were ice cold toward Him, He certainly will not give up on you now.

Next come the questions. Do you trust Him? Do you need Him and follow Him? Are you certain that He loves *you*?

Now respond. Say something. 'Jesus, I need you'—that is always a good response. Or, 'I trust you,' 'I believe you,' 'I follow you,' 'I love you,' or 'thank you.' Just say something.

If you are stuck here, talk to someone else. Ask for help. Ask that person to pray for you. Be honest and open with your doubts. That is a good thing, and it is even more evidence of the Spirit with you.

IS HE STRONG ENOUGH?

Now to the Lord's strength. He is your God of love *and* power.

When His people were afraid, God often gave reminders of His power. For us today, this is an under-used weapon against your anxieties. So here is another story of God's power to people who are anxious and fearful. Try to imagine it. Try to enter in. The New Testament stories want you to be more than a spectator. They are inviting you in as a participant.

There arose a great storm on the sea, so that the boat was being swamped by the waves; but he [Jesus] was asleep. And they went and woke him, saying, 'Save us, Lord; we are perishing.' And he said to them, 'Why are you afraid, O you of little faith?' Then he rose and rebuked the winds and the sea, and there was a great calm. And the men marveled, saying, 'What sort of man is this, that even winds and sea obey him?' (Matt. 8:24-27)

Imagine it. You are in some kind of storm, Jesus says a word and everything is calm. All of a sudden you remember. In the beginning, all creation came into existence by His word. Now the Creator is in your boat. Very close. This could alleviate some anxiety.

A little while later, Jesus met His disciples in a storm, but this time He walked out to them, *on* the water. That is not something you see every day. It could only be done by someone with unusual, more-than-human power.

'It is a ghost!' and they cried out in fear. But immediately Jesus spoke to them, saying, 'Take heart; it is I. Do not be afraid.' (Matt. 14:24-27)

GOOD FEAR AND BAD FEAR

When fears kick in, they crowd everything else out. They can be so loud, so oppressive. You need something even more jolting to refocus you. The benefit of these stories is that, if you enter in, your worries fade for a moment. That's what something amazing does. It draws attention to itself. What was bothering you a second ago is suddenly a distant memory.

The spring before his high school graduation, Frank's parents thought it would be nice to take a family road trip to Niagara Falls. It was the last thing in the world he wanted to do. His mind was filled with exams, looking for summer jobs, a girlfriend, and time with friends. He thought a vacation, at this time, meant the world was going to pass him by. But he had no choice, so off he went. He was not the most pleasant person to be with during the five-hour drive.

Then the family went over a long bridge, and he saw the falls. He was stunned.

Not everyone is amazed by these falls, but he was. He spent the next day watching, enjoying, mesmerized. The trip, for him, was unforgettable.

His many worries? He didn't even think about them during that trip. Amazement makes worries smaller. And, the reality is, God doesn't just distract us from our worries, He asks us to entrust them to Him.

There are two kinds of fears mentioned in the Bible. One is when bad things can happen. The other is when amazing things happen. You want to run from one; you have a hard time taking your eyes off the other. They share the same name because both fears can control you. *One controls you for the worse, one for the better*. In this way, you fight fear with fear.

That's what happened when the disciples saw Jesus walking on the water. As soon as He entered the boat, the winds stopped. 'And those in the boat worshiped him, saying, "Truly you are the Son of God"' (Matt. 14:33).

Your mission is for the Bible's stories of power to become part of you so you have amazement-on-demand. Then you respond. 'Yes, Lord, I believe, and I believe in you.'

There is much more that God says to you, and all the words are very good. They are even beautiful. But you can see what we are doing. We can't just gather all these words together, memorize a few of them, and then be worry-free. Instead, we want to use this opportunity to really listen and respond.

When Jesus says, 'It will be alright,' He is not just trying to make you feel better like a powerless parent might. He is saying to you, 'I'm here.' And all creation listens to His words.

Main Point

Let fear of the Lord drive out fears of the world.

Questions for Reflection

- Feeling awake? You don't need to be a dutiful student who takes notes, at least not right now. Talk to God and to other people. Ask yourself questions. Maybe even argue with what you are reading. Wake up!
- What message from the Bible is sticking? What truths or passages are catching your attention and why?

5. A Walk With God

Imagine a peaceful place—a place where there is no stress. A room that feels safe and comfortable, a beach, a stream, a song, a place in your mind, a person. As good as that place might be, here is a place that is even better.

Jesus invites you for a walk. That might sound like an invitation that works for older people who don't have anything else to do, but a pleasant walk with a dear friend is a good thing for people of any age at any time. In fact, if you let your mind reach back into history, a walk with God was the best part of the Garden of Eden. You were made for such walks.

The conversation on this walk comes from Matthew 6. Since Jesus knows you so well, He jumps right into what is important.

Do not be anxious about your life, what you will eat or what you will drink, nor about your body, what you will put on. (Matt. 6:25)

This sounds like, 'Stop it! Don't be anxious!' But that is not what Jesus is saying.

A little while later He will say words like this to a mother who lost her son. 'Do not weep' (Luke 7:13). He is not telling her to stop crying. He is saying that He has come to comfort and help her. He is saying, 'Take courage. I am here.'

Jesus then identifies some of your anxieties. He starts with the basics—food and clothes. They are things you need. You must have them in order to live. Your life depends on them. You could add to this list your worries that might not be life and death but are important to you. These *feel* like life or death. To you, He might add, 'Don't fret about the friends who aren't speaking to you, the boy who you think doesn't know you exist, tomorrow's exam, a job, a decision about your future, or last night's family row.'

He knows you are anxious, and He knows you will always have your fair share of worries. The most important thing you can do is go for a walk with Him and listen.

Look at the birds of the air: they neither sow nor reap nor gather into barns, and yet your heavenly Father feeds them. Are you not of more value than they? And which of you by

being anxious can add a single hour to his
span of life? And why are you anxious about
clothing? Consider the lilies of the field, how
they grow: they neither toil nor spin, yet I tell
you, even Solomon in all his glory was not
arrayed like one of these. (Matt. 6:26-29)

Look around, Jesus says. Birds. Wildflowers. They are cared for by the one who created them. Now you may be asking, *what does this have to do with my anxiety?*

DOES GOD REALLY CARE?

One spring I saw a nest of baby robins in a small tree behind our house. I first saw the blue eggs, then the protective mother, then hairless blind babies, then downy feathers. All this happened in less than a week. When the babies were in that cute but helpless stage I watched two of them fall out of the nest. The third was actually pushed out by the mother. They needed, I was sure, to be rescued. Cats were close by. What would these helpless birds ever eat? Within about five minutes of them scrambling around like the lost chicks that they were, one flew away, then another, then the third. A moment later they were perched on a wire, looking like all the other self-confident robins, experts at bird life.

God cares for them.

Take a peek in a stream and see this same care. No one feeds the trout that occasionally appear in the pools at the bend. When you see the bottom it looks like, and is, inedible brown muck. But these fish do just fine. God cares for them.

I was walking in the woods recently and realized I would die quickly if I were alone and stranded. I never see anything I could eat, except for the animals I could never catch. Meanwhile, the woods teamed with healthy and well-fed deer, wild turkeys, foxes and who knows what else. Sasquatch?!

If you live in a city, you could consider the pigeons. They are everywhere. God *really* cares for them.

Jesus asks you to think about such things.

Then He surprises you. He asks you a question. You were listening, now He expects you to say something.

Are you not of more value than they?

It is a real question. Go ahead, answer.

'Sort of.'

'Sometimes.'

'I guess so.'

He asks another question. You don't have to answer this one.

Can you worry yourself into an extra hour of life?

He seems to be teasing you a bit. *You* know the answer, *He* knows the answer. It is a very good thing when God is being playful. He is not worried, so maybe you don't have to worry either.

You begin to notice that He is treating you as His child. He is saying that you can't control small matters of life. He never intended you to have so much control. Only your Father can turn back time.

Then He digs beneath your anxiety and makes an observation.

O you of little faith.

The idea is that you aren't very confident that your Father will do what He says. You trust Him for some things, such as how He can bring you to heaven, but not others, such as how He can help you today. But don't worry quite yet about your little speck of faith. Faith the size of a small seed is enough to move mountains. It is not the size of your faith that is so powerful.

It is that your faith is another way of saying, 'I am with Him,' and He can move mountains. Your confidence in Jesus has plenty of time to grow. As it does, expect a few doubts along the way.

All this takes place on a walk. Jesus walks with you and uses creation as a way to teach you of His care. His gentleness, love and strength are on display.

Jesus, thank you for taking me for walks. I am trying to listen.

Main Point

Count your blessings, to remind yourself that God cares.

Questions for Reflection

- How does this walk with Jesus increase your understanding of Him and your trust in Him?
- Have you been able to talk to anyone about these things yet? If not, take a risk and talk with a parent, or talk with a friend.
- Consider going for a walk in your neighborhood, park, woods, etc. Ask God to give you eyes to see the many ways in which He's taking care of needs.

6. Your Wants and Your Fears

Do you ever wish you could grow up faster? Maybe you wish you were in high school. Maybe you wish you were in college. You wish you had a career. You think about being married. You think about having a family. It seems like young people are often in a hurry to move on to the next phase of life.

Let's pause a minute. Here is what you have so far.

1. The Lord says that He is very near. He says that He loves you and He is strong.
2. You respond. You speak to Him and believe.

In other words, when you grow up, you hope to become a child. A child knows she is not very strong. She needs someone else. She cries out when afraid. Children are not overwhelmed by the problems of tomorrow. In fact, children under five usually don't know what *tomorrow* even means. When you don't understand the concept of tomorrow, it is harder to be anxious.

Whoever humbles himself like this child is the greatest in the kingdom of heaven. (Matt. 18:4)

God, I'm not trying to rule the roost, I don't want to be king of the mountain. I haven't meddled where I have no business or fantasized grandiose plans. I've kept my feet on the ground, I've cultivated a quiet heart. Like a baby content in its mother's arms, my soul is a baby content. (Ps. 131:1-2, The Message)

'A baby content.' Or, a child content. Children know they need help. If children need something, they have to ask a parent. But being a child is harder than it looks. Even children have a hard time being children. The ghosts and boogeymen are part of it. But there is more. They also have desires that they want satisfied. They want things, and they freak out when they don't get them.

WANTS AND NEEDS

Your wants and desires are not the same as your needs. You *need* food and clothing. You *want* desert, success, love, attention, acceptance, to be more attractive, video games, and your own version of toys. When these are too important to you, they become burdens that add to your worries and make everything worse. Somehow, those desires must become a little less important.

A young girl was walking down a street and noticed that a neighbor had a little red sports car for sale. In a moment, she saw herself in that car. It had been made for her. She had to have it. For two days she pleaded with her parents to get her that car. She cried, yelled, threatened and accused. She could see herself in the car, and feared that her dream was fading. Her parent's job, she figured, was to serve her by getting her the things that she *needed*. The fact that she was eleven-years-old didn't matter.

You believe that God will take care of your basic necessities. You worry about what you *want* more than what you need, and those wants or desires can drive you mad.

The tricky part of these desires is that they are not necessarily bad. There is nothing wrong with wanting acceptance, success or most things on your list. The problem is *how much* you want them. When a smaller desire isn't met, you are sad. When a really big desire isn't met, life feels like it is over.

What has become your little red sports car? What in your life is to die for?

Do you *want* to be liked by a particular person, or do you *need* to be liked?

Do you *want* a good grade, or do you *need* it?

Would you *like* to be more attractive or more athletic so you can be accepted, or do you *love* being accepted and approved by others?

Once your desires become too big, they should be reduced into regular old desires. If not, God will get smaller to you. After all, He isn't giving you what you need so why bother turning to Him?

WHAT SHOULD I DO?

The demanding child must grow into the content child. And there is a way to do it. It is called '***confession***'. Confession means that you tell the Lord that your desires are getting too big. That's all.

A simple confession can go like this.

God, you are God. I am not. My desires have gotten too big and I don't even know what to do about them.

Or,

Oops, there they go again. I am becoming a demanding child. Please forgive me.

Here are verses you can remember when you think God is not giving you enough of the things you want.

For my thoughts are not your thoughts, neither are your ways my ways, declares the LORD. For as the heavens are higher than the earth, so are my ways higher than your ways and my thoughts than your thoughts. (Isa. 55:8–9)

In response, here is another simple confession.

You know what I need better than I do. But it is really hard not to have some of the things I want.

When your desires have become very big, confess.

When your relationship with the Lord seems distant, it is probably because you are not getting what you want. Confess.

You can't beat confession. It will help you remember that you really do need Jesus. When your desires become more important than God, that is sin. The good part about seeing your sin is that it will remind you that, when Jesus died because of your sins, it was a big deal, because your sin is more of a problem than you think. Another good part about seeing sin is that you discover that the Lord forgives you, loves you and loves having you close, even when you are far from perfect.

Children are heroes in God's house because they know they need help and they call out to their Father. When they throw a hissy-fit, they know their Father will accept them back. Then they settle into a life in which they trust their Father, rest easily because they know that their Father will take care of them, and know that there is plenty they do not understand.

Main Point

Trust God with the desires of your heart.

Questions for Reflection

- Here are words for children. 'Jesus, help me.' 'Thank you.' How will you slip them into your vocabulary today?
- What would you say that you really want? That is where you will find your frustration and your fears. Can you explain the connection between wants-that-are-too-big and fears?
- Think of some things to confess right now. Remember, God welcomes confession from His children.

7. Today

What are you doing tomorrow? Just asking that question, might make your heart beat a little faster. Projects. Deadlines. Papers. Relationships. Stress ... okay, slow down. The Lord is with you. He will care about tomorrow. You only need to be concerned about today.

Six-hundred-thousand people were walking in the desert with only the food and drink they could carry. They would be walking in this same desert for forty years. As their supply ran dry they were definitely anxious. It was the perfect opportunity to cry out to the Lord. A simple 'help!' would have been great. Instead, they grumbled and complained to their leaders. They never even spoke to the Lord (Exod. 16).

But God fed them anyway. A sweet flake would rain down every night. The people called it manna, which is Hebrew for 'what is it?!' No one had ever seen or tasted it before.

The deal was this. Each morning, the people would gather all they needed for that day. They were not to leave any of it for the next day. There would be new manna for tomorrow.

In other words, manna would show if they trusted the Lord. If they stashed away a little extra manna for tomorrow, they trusted in themselves. If they left none for tomorrow morning, they trusted God's words to them— He would care for them tomorrow.

As you can imagine, even though God had shown Himself to these people as loving and strong, and was certainly with them, most of the people hid some extra manna after that first day. By morning, between the horrible smell of decay and the worms, the people learned their lesson. They were not trustworthy, but God was.

You can understand why all this was the perfect way for God to instruct His people. If God gave them enough manna for a week, they would forget about Him until the week was almost over. Then they would do some grumbling, maybe mixed in with a 'help!' or two. They would not learn to be dependent children who needed their Father every day.

DO YOU HAVE 'MANNA' TODAY?

Today the names have changed but the lesson has not. *Manna* pointed to God's *grace*, which He gives you every day. It is more than enough for what we need. *Grace* pointed to the *Spirit* himself. The Spirit is your better-manna who gives you power for today.

Here is a passage you might know. It goes, *ask-seek-knock*. It is about what you need each day. Luke tells you that what you need most is the Spirit, and you can have as much of Him and His power as you ask.

> *[Jesus said] everyone who asks receives, and the one who seeks finds, and to the one who knocks it will be opened. What father among you, if his son asks for a fish, will instead of a fish give him a serpent; or if he asks for an egg, will give him a scorpion? If you then, who are evil, know how to give good gifts to your children, how much more will the heavenly Father give the Holy Spirit to those who ask him! (Luke 11:10-13)*

Today, not tomorrow. That is what is important. Today the Lord is with you by His Spirit. *He* will worry about tomorrow. You deal with what is in front of you.

Many cities have horse-drawn carriages as a way for tourists to see the sights. These horses usually have blinders. They allow horses to see what is in front of them but nothing else. Blinders send a message from the driver to the horse. 'Don't be alarmed by that engine noise next to you. You are alright. Just look straight ahead. Keep walking. You are doing fine. I'll worry about the cars and busses.'

There are human versions of blinders, too, for people who get distracted by others when they are working. Human blinders look goofy but they seem to help.

Your job is to put on blinders. All the stuff that distracts you? God cares about those things. They are His job, not yours. Your job is what is in front of you. When you yank off your blinders and get upset about tomorrow, *you are imagining tomorrow without God in it.* You are thinking like an orphan who has no loving and strong Father. The truth is that the Spirit is helping you *now.* You have everything you need now. You are not yet prepared for tomorrow. Instead, when you wake up tomorrow, you will ask Him for manna, for grace, for more of His Spirit. You will ask Him for help, and He will help you.

Here is something amazing. God partners with you. Jesus describes it as though He is the ox who is pulling the heavy burdens of your life. He invites you to be yoked to Him and pull along with Him, though He, of course, is doing most of the work (Matt 11:29). Since you are a mere mortal, your work is limited to what is in front of you. He doesn't ask you to control the things that you can't control.

You partner with Him in the work today. He has control over tomorrow, and He will help you to partner when the time comes.

And which of you by being anxious can add a single hour to his span of life? If then you are not able to do as small a thing as that, why are you anxious about the rest? (Luke 12:25-26)

A teacher announced, 'Tomorrow you will have a test on the periodic table of elements.'

Everybody in the class looked at each other and started whispering, 'How can he do that? I don't know anything about that. We are sure to fail.'

'Trust me,' said the teacher, 'I will make sure you have the help you need. Just do the homework that I assigned—you can begin working on that now.'

During the rest of the day, some did the homework, some complained about the test scheduled for the next day for which they were unprepared. That evening, some students couldn't sleep, some slept well because they believed their teacher.

When the next day arrived, the teacher unveiled a large periodic table, explained how it was arranged, and provided a list that identified the full names of all the elements. Then he handed out some questions for the 'test.' But it was a peculiar test. The teacher himself guided them to the right answers until everyone understood and passed.

If you worry about tomorrow, you imagine it without knowing how the teacher—Jesus, in your case—will give you what you need. You will, instead, be absolutely sure that you won't be able to handle it. And you are almost right. You don't have to handle it *today*. You have help for other things today, such as help with your homework or stress over your girlfriend/ boyfriend. Your job is to listen to your teacher and trust Him for tomorrow.

This, of course, will not be easy. You are learning a new skill that comes from trusting Jesus. You are erecting a barrier in your mind between today and tomorrow. But you will find all kinds of ways to scale that wall, dig under it or breach it. The anxious and fearful mind is busy, and no matter how much you tell it to stay put, it keeps finding a way to escape into tomorrow.

You have plenty of time to learn.

Main Point

Leave tomorrow in God's hands.

Questions for Reflection

- How would you summarize what you have heard so far? Does it make you hopeful? What is especially interesting to you?
- Your ability to stay focused on today depends on you being able to find something that is worthy of your attention. What do you imagine could be important enough to keep you in the present rather than the future?

8. Anxiety Left to Itself

Why bother working on your fears and worries? Take a moment to gather together some reasons.

1. An obvious reason is that anxieties will always be part of life. Sports tryouts, dating relationships, friendships, tests, and public speaking—these are everyday occurrences that are ripe for anxiety. Not only are they common, but we all need help with issues like this. The good news is, you are getting help. The skills you are learning now are ones that most adults didn't have at your age. Many adults do not have them *now*. You are learning spiritual skills that will change the course of your life.

2. Another reason is that these skills apply to most every problem in life: knowing that Jesus is close, talk to Him, and focus on today, not tomorrow. You can use these

skills when you face almost anything in life that is painful or difficult.

3. If you *do not* deal with the many cares of life, God will become less important to you, and your anxieties will get worse. Here are some of those details.

ANXIETY CAN MAKE YOU DEAF TO THE WORDS OF JESUS

A college student's world was getting smaller. Anxiety was keeping him from being around other people, which makes college life impossible. A crowded classroom was becoming too uncomfortable. He couldn't concentrate on his work. He would have to drop out for the semester if things didn't change fast. On a weekend visit home, his parents took him to talk with his pastor.

'Here is a passage where Jesus talks to you about your anxieties.' The pastor used the verses about Jesus and His walk with an anxious person. He had barely said anything when the young man responded.

'I've tried that.'

The student hadn't heard a word. Anxiety wants a quick answer, and he didn't think God's words would do any magic. His next stop was to a physician who would prescribe some medication. That helped, but not enough to finish the semester. This is not to say that medicine cannot be helpful or that there may be times for medicine but, in the case of this story, he missed an opportunity to learn more about Jesus and learn important life skills.[1]

Jesus told this story. It gives a reason to listen to Him when we are worried.

A sower was throwing out seed. Jesus Himself is the sower. Some seeds fell to the ground and grew. In other words, people listened and believed. Other seed fell on hearts that were not interested in listening, and that seed didn't bear fruit, the words of Jesus didn't matter.

Others [other seeds] are the ones sown among thorns. They are those who hear the word, but the cares of the world and the deceitfulness of riches and the desires for other things enter in and choke the word, and it proves unfruitful. (Mark 4:18-19)

'The cares of the world' are your worries and anxieties—popularity, athletic or academic

---

1   Medicine is often a touchy subject, so I want to handle this with sensitivity. If you sense your anxiety is to that level, seek out your parents, a trusted pastor or adult, and consult your doctor.

success, body image and outer appearance; just to name a few. They are not wrong but they can be dangerous if you ignore what Jesus says. If you don't listen to Him, your anxieties will 'choke the word.' You will be deaf to His words of life because you think you know better. Life, you figured, could be found in other places.

What can you do? Listen, really listen. Respond to what Jesus says to you.

Remember that listening is not natural. What is natural is that you try to ignore the cares of the world because you don't think there is anything you can do about them. So you try to tough it out. ***But if you don't listen to Jesus you will be less alive.*** Jesus, after all, is life itself. He created life and brings life. His words bring life. Ignore His words and that life in you begins to fade.

You, on the other hand, are trying to head toward the Life. You want to listen. You might not think that such a small step is a big deal, but your willingness to listen is a massive sign that you are very alive. You can be sure the Spirit is giving you power.

This story is a helpful warning. It gives you a reason to keep at it. When you are anxious, listen to Jesus. Don't stop listening until Jesus' words sound very good.

ANXIETY CAN LEAD TO INNOCENT DISTRACTIONS THAT ARE NOT ALWAYS INNOCENT

When we don't listen to what Jesus says about 'the cares of the world,' we still do *something*. We usually try to find some innocent distractions. What makes them innocent is that you wouldn't be too embarrassed if a parent saw you doing them. You might call these distractions 'entertainment.'

Music
Social media
Television, movies, websites
Video games
Fantasy novels
Shopping
Getting out of the house

It is curious that homework and more productive activities are rarely used as distractions. One reason they are not your favorite distractions is that these activities need careful, active concentration, and anxiety interferes with that kind of focus. Anxiety prefers something a little more mindless. Movies, for example, are usually mindless. They often don't ask anything of you.

What about video games? They certainly need your attention. You are so focused that you have to remember to blink. But this attention is different than what you would bring to a job or homework. With video games you are drawn into an alternative world that is happening around you. They are mindless yet intense. That is a perfect combination for avoiding your anxieties in your real world. Even better, in that alternative world you have special power. You have control. If you fail, you get a do-over. You can see why they are so addictive.

You might have heard how more and more people are saying that we need to unplug ourselves. With so much noise you have no time to consider important matters, and you have no idea how to rest. You are already a step ahead on these things. But you still might consider times to unplug. Twenty minutes? An hour? You already have biblical material that can get you thinking while taking a break from your entertainment. You might even consider a personal journal as a way to slow down and consider real life.

ANXIETY CAN LEAD TO LESS INNOCENT DISTRACTIONS THAT ARE DANGEROUS

Innocent distractions usually don't stay innocent for very long. If small doses of entertainment distract you from the cares of the world, then large doses, you would think, will distract you better. If two hours of video games are a fine distraction from life, six hours are better.

Social media is even easier. You can spend as much time as you have to give. Then, when you *have to* face your responsibilities, social media provides interruptions and brief diversions along the way.

With all the commotion, you don't notice that you are being changed. Your anxieties are multiplying, and the worst anxiety of all is coming to get you.

Beware of the fear of boredom.

The anxiety of nothingness. You feel dead without entertainment. Your life must have a constant soundtrack.

Depression, for many people, is life with distractions that don't work anymore. What's left is dread, dread that the future will be empty.

Drugs and alcohol soon become essential parts of entertainment and distraction. Perhaps porn brings a hint of life for a moment.

Distractions become less innocent. These are the ones you don't want other people to see.

Why bother with all this? You have good reasons to keep listening. Life is lived best when you look at it closely and listen to the Lord. That's what wise people do. When you read what is called the wisdom books of the Bible, especially Proverbs and Ecclesiastes, they take us into a careful look at how to live and how not to live. When you look carefully at anxiety and fear, you discover there is one of two ways to go. You can listen to the Lord and learn about peace and rest, or you can avoid Him and feel better for a moment, but it ends badly.

Here is the good news. If you have slid into dangerous distractions, the way out can start now. Keep reading. Respond.

Main Point

Don't let anxiety lead you into sin.

Questions for Reflection

- What reasons do you have for listening to the Lord about your worries?

- What cautions do you have about your entertainment? Has boredom come knocking yet?
- Are you indulging in dangerous distractions? Confess to the Lord and seek help from someone in your church.

9. Living Now

At this point you may be thinking, *I know I should focus on today but that's easier said than done.* And, you'd be exactly right, but that's how much of life is. We know certain things, but applying them and living by them is different. So, let's take some time thinking more about how we can live in this way.

Just a reminder, the Lord says two things to you: He is with you, and, since He will worry about tomorrow, focus on today. Let's consider more carefully that skill of living today.

It starts with a mission.

For we are his workmanship, created in Christ Jesus for good works, which God prepared beforehand, that we should walk in them. (Eph. 2:10)

You are not your own, for you were bought with a price. (1 Cor. 6:19-20)

You have a God-given job. The job is not that difficult. In fact, it is good. Work itself is not bad. However, work that you don't like makes you wish you were on permanent vacation. Someone who enjoys construction might not like sitting all day at a computer. Someone who likes to work quickly and independently might not be suited to being a teacher. But God's work for you is good, and He promises to give you everything you need to do it. His Spirit will equip you.

A lot of your life is already mapped out. During the week, you wake up, have whatever morning routine you have, go to school or work or look for work, talk with friends, check phones. All of a sudden, your day is more than half over. Then you probably have other routines. You can go through a lot of life without thinking about who you are and where you are going. You have your routines and some of them aren't going to change too much, at least not now.

Yet there are a few things that you can insert.

FIRST THINGS FIRST

Begin here: is there any awkwardness in your relationship with Jesus? Are you feeling guilty about anything? Are you keeping Him at a distance because you fear He might not let you do what you want to do? Do you keep Him at a distance because you are planning to sin? If so, you might think, why bother talking to Him now? I might as well wait until I'm ready to get serious.

No matter why you feel awkward, talk to Him. The Lord never turns His back on those who come to Him. Just speak honestly. Tell Him your dilemma. Ask forgiveness and be assured He forgives. Ask Him for help. Say *something*.

If you get stuck here, ask another person for help. The more words you can speak about this, the better. Behind the scenes is a spiritual battle in which Satan says, wait until you are good, then you can talk to Jesus. The truth, of course, is that we come to Jesus because we are *not* good. Any reasons that keep you from speaking to Jesus have Satan's fingerprints all over them.

Here are his more common lies.

You are too bad.
Jesus is ticked off with you.
God is trying to keep you from having fun.

Don't believe them.

LOCATE YOUR ANXIETIES
Now go back to your daily routines again. Where do you notice that stresses and anxieties enter in? Those are the places you want to pause.

Name them. What are those anxieties? What are you predicting will happen?

Talk about them. Talk, at least, to the Lord. You could include a parent too.

Next, zoom into today. That's where you have grace from the Spirit. That's where you will receive courage. Here are ways to do that.

PREPARE TODAY, FOR TOMORROW

Tomorrow might be waiting with a decision to make, a test, or a difficult conversation. You could prepare today by getting the advice of someone who has experience in what you face. That person could give some direction on how to prepare. If you already know what to do, such as study for an exam, then you can get to it.

LOVE SOMEONE

Keep looking at what is in front of you. Look especially at the *people* who are right in front of you. The Spirit who works in you has a special interest in your day-to-day relationships. Some of the good things He gives you are love, patience, kindness and gentleness (Gal 5:22-23). You use these with the people around you.

Are you grumpy or easily frustrated? That is important. You can deal with that right now. Ask forgiveness of those who had to witness it.

You can let them know that you are anxious about something, but that is no excuse to be cantankerous (that's a fun word that just means grumpy or irritable).

Is there a relationship with a friend that is a mess? What can you do now to mend it? Ask forgiveness for your part of the mess.

Do you avoid people where you live? Move in their direction rather than demand your own privacy. Ask someone about his or her own life.

Your primary job is to love. You have been loved by Jesus, so you love. Look around and take an interest in someone.

WORK

As you look right in front of you, notice the small jobs that you have avoided. Does a room need to be cleaned? Are you putting off looking for work? Have you said you would do something but haven't done it? If you said 'yes, I'll do that,' but your actions have said, 'no,' you have lied. Lying, of course, breaks relationships and it is evidence that Satan has some influence in your life because he is *The* Liar. So today, do what you said you would do. If that is impossible, then ask the person's forgiveness for saying you would do something that you could not do.

The work that you have today might seem ordinary. But when you do *anything* because Jesus calls you to do it, you are doing something important. So put down your phone, get up from your chair and do something that you have put off.

DO WHAT IS RIGHT

Anxiety comes when you do the wrong thing, peace comes when you do what is right and good. Proverbs put it this way.

The wicked flee when no one pursues, but the righteous are bold as a lion (Prov. 28:1).

The righteous ask, what does God say is right and good right now? Then they aim to do it.

During the plane hijackings of September 11, 2001, the heroes were those people who knew what was right to do. They went into buildings rather than away from them, because that was their duty as firefighters. They attacked hijackers when they knew such an attack would mean their death, because they knew it was right to stop hijackers before they killed many more people.

The heroes of the Bible handled their anxieties in the same way. What was right? What has God told me to do? You have probably seen examples of that among your friends. Somebody stood against a bully, even though there could have been a price to pay. Someone simply said, 'I don't think we should do that,' even though peers could mock.

God calls this discernment—knowing the difference between right and wrong. It comes when you are willing to learn the difference and practice it.

If you want to go a little deeper on this, keep track of your conscience. It can help you identify what is wrong through what you hide. If you are hiding things, you will be anxious. It can also identify what is wrong when you feel guilty. If you keep doing those things, you will be anxious. You will do best if you listen to your conscience rather than ignore it. Your conscience is trying to tell you something. It prefers that you are bold as a lion instead of running away in fear.

As a general rule, ask someone to help you when your conscience bothers you. Think of someone you trust and can provide wise counsel. Contact that person. Today. This would be an example of great courage.

ADJUST YOUR BLINDERS

Meanwhile, tomorrow will keep sneaking into today. Sometimes it seems as though there is nothing you can do to get it to leave. But you might have more power than you think. Try pushing tomorrow into where it belongs. Put your blinders on. Readjust them. Put up a fight against tomorrow by trusting that your Father will give you His Spirit of power when you need Him.

Yet, even after all this, there will be days when your worries seem to take over. You will feel so weak. At those times, don't think for a minute that God has left you, or that He is disappointed. He is strong for you. He cares for you and your future when you are asleep. He will certainly care for you when you are tired and overwhelmed.

Main Point

Face today boldly, in the power of His Spirit.

Questions for Reflection

- What step will you take today?
- Who might you talk to about it?

10. Courage and Rest

Soldiers will tell you that they are afraid. They enter into danger, but they are afraid. Courage is not the absence of fear and anxiety. Courage is doing what is good, right and important even when you are afraid. Courage is knowing that God is with you and then following through on your mission.

GIDEON'S FEAR

Gideon, a soldier, might encourage you. An angel of the Lord visited him. 'The LORD is with you, O mighty man of valor' (Judg. 6:12). With that introduction, you can guess that he was afraid. 'The LORD is with you'—that is the first thing God says to people who are afraid.

'O mighty man of valor'? Gideon was *not* bold or courageous. He was threshing wheat indoors, which might not seem like a big deal until you know that when you thresh wheat you are separating the useful parts from the waste, and you need a small breeze to do it. Gideon should have been outdoors, but was hiding from enemies who might show up and take whatever they wanted.

Gideon replied, 'but if the LORD is with us, why has all this happened to us? ... The LORD has abandoned us into the hand of Midian' (Judg. 6:13, NIV).

At least he spoke honestly.

The angel turned out to be Jesus. He is the Lord.

The LORD turned to him and said, 'Go in the strength you have and save Israel out of Midian's hand. Am I not sending you?' (Judg. 6:14, NIV).

In other words, the enemy is so weak and scared that you could fight them on your own, even if I—the Lord—wasn't with you. (But I will be with you).

Gideon responded. He said that his entire clan was weak, and he was the weakest among them. His valor and courage were definitely not on display.

A little later the Lord told Gideon to tear down an idol that his father had made. This would get the people one step closer to being ready for battle. Gideon did as the Lord asked, but he did it at night so no one would know it was him. This was definitely courage, but courage does not always feel very courageous.

Gideon needed tons of reassurances and some pushing and prodding along the way. He was always looking for a way out of his duty. When he finally went into battle, he routed the enemy with a small group of three hundred men, armed only with torches and trumpets. Today he is considered an Old Testament hero.

The reason Gideon can encourage you is that he was so human, so weak, so reluctant, so afraid, even when God was so clearly with him. It's like reading a story about yourself.

The Lord says to *you*, 'The Lord is with you, O mighty man of valor.' 'The Lord is with you, O mighty woman of valor.'

The courage to do what the Lord says comes from His Spirit. As 'the Spirit of the LORD clothed Gideon' (Judg. 6:34), so you too are clothed with the Lord. The Lord knows that the hard things in your day are not for cowards. So He gives you Himself—Jesus-your-warrior—

and predicts that you too will be a person of boldness and courage. If you continue to listen to and talk with Him, this is a *true* prediction of your future.

GOD'S ARMOR

The apostle Paul wrote that your enemies are much more serious than the flesh-and-blood soldiers Gideon had to face. Your enemy is greater than the disapproval of friends and classmates. Your enemies are dark, spiritual powers who follow the devil (Eph. 6:10-20), and they are usually right behind the things that make you worry.

When you worry about being rejected by a friend, your real enemies whisper to you, just out of sight. They tell you that your life will be over if your friend doesn't like you. You will have no reason to live.

When you worry about what you are going to do after you graduate, they assure you that God is not really with you. Even if He were, they say, He wouldn't help you anyway because He is interested in people who are more obedient than you.

Here is the truth. When you believe Jesus and trust Him, even with a little bit of faith, He covers you. You are prepared for today with bullet-proof protection from head to foot. A helmet of salvation. A chest covering that Jesus Himself wore—it assures you that everything that was His is now yours, so you can be sure that you are forgiven and loved. Shoes that proclaim peace. A sword that is the Spirit's power. All of this is because of Jesus. When He died for sins, He did more than you think. You are totally protected and strengthened.

Can you see that protection? You have it. Believe what God says and look with eyes of faith. Can you imagine what a mighty person of valor would do now that you are dressed for anything? Go slow, little steps are fine. Gideon began with small steps.

REST

People of valor and courage also need rest. That too is part of your job.

When you have no one to help you, you can't rest. Anxiety is always busy. Your mind never stops or you are striving to make something happen. Once you get to sleep, even your dreams are stories of anxiety and the pressures of life. You just don't seem to escape them. But children can rest. They know their limitations and they trust parents to care for them.

Children can hear some parental noise around the house as they are falling asleep. A muffled conversation. Someone safe who is cleaning up the debris of the day. They are comforted that someone who loves them is present and awake.

Behold, he who keeps Israel will neither slumber nor sleep. (Ps. 121:4)

Jesus wants you to learn how to rest.

Come to me, all who labor and are heavy laden, and I will give you rest. Take my yoke upon you, and learn from me, for I am gentle and lowly in heart, and you will find rest for your souls. For my yoke is easy, and my burden is light. (Matt. 11:28-30)

The rest Jesus gives you is a certain kind of rest, even deeper than a good night's sleep. The rest He gives is from always trying to prove yourself and measure up to others or measure up to what God tells you to do. You can't rescue yourself by being good and obeying more laws. Obedience is good, but it will never give you rest. You can rest because Jesus obeyed for you. He was perfect in His thoughts, words, and deeds. He didn't just forgive you, He gave you His achievements and His obedience. Everything that is His is now yours. He obeyed for you, as if you had obeyed. He then took all of your sin on Himself at the cross. You are right because of His righteousness and atoning death. Your most important mission is to rest in what Jesus has done for you.

In returning and rest you shall be saved; in quietness and in trust shall be your strength. (Isa. 30:15)

Faith, trust, rest, believe—these are all ways of saying that Jesus has done all the work. He has loved you, forgiven you, and obeyed where you did not. You have life because you rest in His life and what He did.

From there, you can become a rest expert.

Prayer is rest, so is listening closely to a sermon, not having anything to prove to your friends, asking someone for help, talking to the Lord without even asking anything, listening carefully to *anyone* (anxiety usually doesn't listen very well), enjoying time with a person or a meal or a class or a book or anything in creation, laughing at yourself, laughing at something funny that doesn't put anyone down, getting to know someone else a little better, seeing good in people, learning about the Sabbath, hanging out with your family, as well as actually going to bed at a decent time.

Go ahead, practice rest. It is all part of your job. You are protected, God is wide awake, and He will give you courage again tomorrow. If tomorrow comes and you are not as successful as you hoped, remember that you trust in Him more than you trust in your own success. Then believe that He is with you, figure out what you can do that is right and good today, and practice rest.

Main Point

God calls us to rest in Him.

Questions for Reflection

- What do you think about the truth that your enemy the devil is an even more serious concern than any of your fears?
- What might rest look like for you?

Appendix A: What Now?

- Keep in mind what the Lord says to anxious, pressured people: (1) I am with you, (2) you have the Spirit who gives you strength for today.

- Find a Bible passage that reminds you that the Lord is very strong.

- Find a Bible passage that assures you that the Lord loves you.

- Your doubts about God are very important. Gideon, for example, had doubts. Talk to the Lord about them, and talk to a trusted friend, pastor or family member about them.

- Your doubts about yourself are very important. Does your soul feel dead and unaffected by what God says? Are you reluctant to follow Him because you fear that you have to give up something important to you? Do you think you are too bad to hear things this good? Gideon had these doubts too. '"But LORD," Gideon asked, "how can I save Israel? My clan is the weakest in Manasseh, and I am the least in my family"' (Judg. 6:15). Talk to the Lord, and talk to another person.

- Write a short list of how you can focus on today rather than be pulled into tomorrow.

- Answer the 'Questions for Reflection.'

- Your goal is not to be free of all worry. That won't happen. Your goal is to listen and talk to the Lord when are you anxious. 'Pour out' you heart to Him (Ps. 62:8). Talk to Him as you would a friend.

- Tell your friends that you read a book about anxiety. Ask them if they want to read it and talk about it together.

Appendix B: Other Books on this Topic

BOOKLETS ON FEAR, WORRY AND ANXIETY

Baker, Amy. *Social Anxiety: Being Comfortable in Your Own Skin* (New Growth Press, 2011).

Jones, Robert. *Why Worry?: Getting to the Heart of Your Anxiety* (P&R Publishing, 2018).

Powlison, David. *Worry: Pursuing a Better Path to Peace* (P&R Publishing, 2012).

Wallace, Jocelyn. *Anxiety and Panic Attacks: Trusting God When You're Afraid* (New Growth Press, 2013).

BOOKS ON FEAR, WORRY AND ANXIETY

Fitzpatrick, Elyse. *Overcoming Fear, Worry, and Anxiety: Becoming a Woman of Faith and Confidence* (Harvest House Publishers, 2001).

Perritt, John. *Insecure: Fighting Our Lesser Fears with a Greater One* (Christian Focus Publications, 2019).

Welch, Edward. *A Small Book for the Anxious Heart: Meditations on Fear, Worry and Trust* (New Growth Press, 2019).

Welch, Edward. *Running Scared: Fear, Worry and the God of Rest* (New Growth Press, 2007).

Welch, Edward. *When I Am Afraid: A Step-by-Step Guide away from Fear and Anxiety* (Evangelical Press, 2010).

Welch, Edward. *When People Are Big and God Is Small* (P&R Publishing, 1997).

Witmer, Timothy. *Mindscape: What to Think About Instead of Worrying* (New Growth Press, 2014).

BOOKS ON EMOTIONS
Groves, Alasdair and Winston Smith. *Untangling Emotions* (Crossway, 2019).

BOOKS ON SPIRITUAL ARMOR
Duguid, Ian. *The Whole Armor of God: How Christ's Victory Strengthens Us for Spiritual Warfare* (Crossway, 2019).

Powlison, David. *Safe and Sound: Standing Firm in Spiritual Battles* (New Growth Press, 2019).

BOOKS OF THE BIBLE
Ecclesiastes; 2 Timothy.

PODCASTS
CCEF.org 'Panic Attacks: A Counseling Case Study' numbers 1-5.

Watch out for other forthcoming books in the
Track series, including:

LIGON DUNCAN
& JOHN PERRITT

A STUDENT'S GUIDE TO

SANCTIFICATION

TRACK
DOCTRINE

A Student's Guide to Sanctification

LIGON DUNCAN & JOHN PERRITT

Knowing that we have been saved by what Jesus has done rather than by what we have done is amazing. But how does this knowledge affect the way we live? What's the point in being good if we will be forgiven anyway? Actually the Bible says that God's forgiveness frees us to live for Him and through the Holy Spirit we can grow to become more and more like Jesus. Ligon Duncan and John Perritt dive into what that means in this short book.

978-1-5271-0451-8

JOHN
PERRITT

TRACK
CULTURE

A STUDENT'S GUIDE TO
TECHNOLOGY

A Student's Guide to Technology

John Perritt

Technology can be a great gift. It allows us to communicate with people all over the world instantly. But it can also do great harm if not used wisely. This short book gives helpful suggestions for how to use technology to glorify God in our lives, as well as making us aware of what dangers there are in misusing technology.

978-1-5271-0449-5

Reformed Youth Ministries (RYM) exists to reach students for Christ and equip them to serve. Passing the faith on to the next generation has been RYM's passion since it began. In 1972 three youth workers who shared a passion for biblical teaching to youth surveyed the landscape of youth ministry conferences. What they found was an emphasis on fun and games, not God's Word. Therefore, they started a conference that focused on the preaching and teaching of God's Word. Over the years RYM has grown beyond conferences into three areas of ministry: conferences, training, and resources.

- **Conferences:** RYM's youth conferences take place in the summer at a variety of locations across the United States and are continuing to expand. We also host parenting conferences throughout the year at local churches.

- **Training:** RYM launched an annual Youth Leader Training (YLT) conference in 2008. YLT has grown steadily through the years and is offered in multiple locations. RYM also offers a Church Internship Program in partnering local churches as well as youth leader coaching and youth ministry consulting.
- **Resources:** RYM offers a variety of resources for leaders, parents, and students. Several Bible studies are offered as free downloads with more titles regularly being added to their catalogue. RYM hosts multiple podcasts: *Parenting Today*, *The Local Youth Worker*, & *The RYM Student Podcast* – all of which can be downloaded on multiple formats. There are many additional ministry tools available for download on the website.

If you are passionate for passing the faith on to the next generation, please visit www.rym.org to learn more about Reformed Youth Ministries. If you are interested in partnering with us in ministry, please visit www.rym.org/donate.

Christian Focus Publications

Our mission statement —

STAYING FAITHFUL

In dependence upon God we seek to impact the world
through literature faithful to His infallible Word, the Bible.
Our aim is to ensure that the Lord Jesus Christ is presented as
the only hope to obtain forgiveness of sin, live a useful life and
look forward to heaven with Him.

Our books are published in four imprints:

CHRISTIAN
FOCUS

Popular works including biographies, commentaries, basic doctrine and Christian living.

CHRISTIAN
HERITAGE

Books representing some of the best material from the rich heritage of the church.

MENTOR

Books written at a level suitable for Bible College and seminary students, pastors, and other serious readers. The imprint includes commentaries, doctrinal studies, examination of current issues and church history.

CF4•K

Children's books for quality Bible teaching and for all age groups: Sunday school curriculum, puzzle and activity books; personal and family devotional titles, biographies and inspirational stories — because you are never too young to know Jesus!

Christian Focus Publications Ltd,
Geanies House, Fearn, Ross-shire,
IV20 1TW, Scotland, United Kingdom.
www.christianfocus.com
blog.christianfocus.com